BE ENCOURAGED

POETRY BOOK

The Lord is my ...

STRENGTH
HOPE
ETERNITY
PEACE
HEALER
EXODUS
REFUGE
DELIVERER

LISA BRADLEY

ISBN: 978-1-943409-68-6

Pure Thoughts Publishing, LLC. Conyers, GA 30013

www.purethoughtspublishing.com

Printed in the United States of America

Table of Contents

BECAUSE YOU WERE HIDDEN 7

BLESS YOUR PEOPLE 9

FREE TO BE BROKEN 11

JEHOVAH IS HIS NAME 13

LIVING IN THE PAST 15

MAN VS GOD 17

RESTING IN COMFORTABLE.............. 19

SPEAK IT.. 23

THE LORD IS 25

THE POWER OF THE OIL 26

The Power of the Oil II 28

VICTIM TO VICTOR 31

YOUR SEASON IS NOW 33

About The Author 35

DEDICATION

"So encourage each other and build each other up, just as you are already doing." (1 Thessalonians 5:11)

I dedicate this book to every person that reads it and my prayer is that you are inspired, uplifted and most of all *ENCOURAGED*.

ACKNOWLEDGMENT

I acknowledgment and thank God for all He has done for me. For without Him none of this would be possible. I will forever be grateful to Him for allowing me to share with the world what He gifted me with. God is truly deserving of all the honor and praise. He is worthy.

BECAUSE YOU WERE HIDDEN

They couldn't see you
Because you were hidden

They couldn't trouble you
Because you were hidden

They couldn't falsely accuse you
Because you were hidden

They couldn't move you
Because you were hidden

They couldn't disrupt your peace
Because you were hidden

They couldn't touch your family
Because you were hidden

They couldn't steal your mind
Because you were hidden

They couldn't take your joy
Because you were hidden

They couldn't destroy you
Because you were hidden

Lisa Bradley
BE ENCOURAGED

They couldn't stifle your praise
Because you were hidden

God had you camouflaged
You were buried in plain sight
Top secret and concealed
But now you are about to stand upright

All because you were hidden

BLESS YOUR PEOPLE

Bless your people Lord
As they lift their hands to worship you
Give them strength and determination
To know that you will see them through

Bless your people Lord
As they struggle with pain
Show them that you are the answer
And with you eternal life they will gain

Bless your people Lord
As they cry out to you in tears
Let them know that you are able
To chase away all of their fears

Bless your people Lord
As they fight these battles within
Remind them that your Word
Is the only weapon needed to win

Bless your people Lord
As they walk through open doors
Let them see your ultimate power
And all you have in store

Bless your people Lord

Lisa Bradley
BE ENCOURAGED

Open their minds to see
To live the life you gave them
Prayer is the key

Bless your people Lord
As they put all of their trust in you and not
man
Give them what they need to fight on
And never turn back as they journey through
this land

FREE TO BE BROKEN

Free me from the guilt and pain I feel
Free me from the heartache and hurt that
won't heal

Free me from the feeling of embarrassment
and shame
Free me from the internal struggle of blame

Free me from any responsibility I thought I
played
Free me from any error in judgment I thought
I made

Free me from the mind restraints I cannot
release
Free me from the firm grip of my inner peace

Free me from the feeling of not having done
enough
Free me from the feeling of inadequacy and
not measuring up

Free me from the resentment that consumes
me

Lisa Bradley
BE ENCOURAGED

Free me from the bitterness that just won't let
me be

Free me from the circumstances and baggage
of the past
Free me from the loves and friendships that
did not last

Free me from the cracked pieces of my
broken soul
Free me from thinking I didn't deserve to be
mended whole

Free me from the desire to want to die in my
brokenness
Free me from thinking I had to settle for so
much less

Free me to forgive myself and others for what
they said and did
Free me to allow myself to be okay in the end

Free me to be what God called me to be
Free me, free all of me, free me from me

JEHOVAH IS HIS NAME

The Lord will provide
I call Him Jehovah-Jireh

The Lord will heal
I call Him Jehovah-Rapha

The Lord is present
I call Him Jehovah-Shammah

The Lord will give me peace
I call Him Jehovah-Shalom

The Lord is my victor
I call Him Jehovah-Nissi

The Lord is righteous
I call Him Jehovah-Tsidkenu

The Lord sanctifies and sets apart
I call Him Jehovah-M'Kaddesh

The Lord is my Shepherd
I call Him Jehovah-Rohi

The Lord will repay
I call Him Jehovah-Gmolah

Lisa Bradley
BE ENCOURAGED

I call Him Jehovah
Jehovah is His Name

LIVING IN THE PAST

When God has delivered us
From situations long ago
We tend to want to hold on to them
And in turn our happiness doesn't grow

Because we've in fact yet to let go
Of the old scars and wounds
Knowing deep down inside
Without doing so we will never truly have room

For the complete fullness of His will
He would have for our lives
For we then fall prey to unforgiveness
That the heart harbors deep inside

The heaviness of this weight
Puts a beating on our soul
It becomes hard to let it loose
Leaving us with anger we cannot control

Masking and covering the bruises
Instead of giving it all to Him
That light that is supposed to shine so bright
Has now become dull and dim

So I encourage you to presently live

Lisa Bradley
BE ENCOURAGED

Do not delay leaving your past
God can cure what ails you
To Him all your cares you can cast

MAN VS GOD

Man …..
    You cannot have what you do not see
God …..
    Speak it as if you already have it

Man …..
    You cannot have the position
God …..
    Promotion comes from me

Man …
    You need to look like me
God …..
    I created you in my image

Man …..
    You cannot have the house or car
God …..
    Delight in me and I will give you the
desires of your heart

Man …..
    You will not be forgiven
God …..
    All you have to do is ask

Man reminds us of our faults

Lisa Bradley
BE ENCOURAGED

God says in Him old things are gone
Man treats us as we were
God says in Him all things are new

I am glad God has delivered me from man

RESTING IN COMFORTABLE

Fear will cause us to stay in familiarity
And in turn have us running away from our
true destiny

That person, that thing, that place that is no
longer
Serves no use and keeps us from growing
stronger

When worry stops us from forging ahead
We then retreat back to what kept us bound
instead

God knows that in order to get us what we
need
He has to make what made us comfortable
not succeed

When we call that individual and they won't
pick up the phone
Or answer the knock on the door when we
visit their home

That club or lounge or hangout spot
Where it used to be lit is now not so hot

Lisa Bradley
BE ENCOURAGED

When we have outgrown these things or have
gotten too relaxed
God then makes them unavailable or hard to
reach to keep us from going back

We cannot rest in our comforts and expect to
walk in purpose
That is why God made uncomfortable a part
of His plan for us

We cannot become stagnant, miss out and get
left behind
Just because God is challenging and
preparing us to be at the front of the line

He is priming and equipping us to get out of
our comfort zone
But know He is not going to give us the
dream and then leave us all alone

The pathway has been paved and the road has
been made clear
He has already placed inside us what we need
to get us there

We cannot allow not knowing the details of
how, where and when
Keep us from living by faith and fulfilling our
God ordained vision

Lisa Bradley
BE ENCOURAGED

We all have free choice but let's just keep it
real
It's much easier and better on us to conform
to His will

We all know that once we decide to live for
Christ
All hell breaks loose and the enemy wants us
to think twice

But no one said when we give our lives to the
Lord
That living easy would be our only reward

We are all going to have a season of conflict
and testing
We just have to stay armored up and not let
satan catch us resting

Oh the devil is very good at his occupation
But that doesn't mean we use that as
justification

To lay dormant, sit in idleness and
complacency
God has so much for us but we have to
envision it spiritually

Seeing it in the natural will only cause us to
lose focus

Lisa Bradley
BE ENCOURAGED

Then we will never be truly ready for what
God has for us

So the challenge now becomes are we ready
to step into God's mission
Or give up and turn away from all that He has
to offer, what's your decision

SPEAK IT

Greater is my portion
Life and death is in my tongue
I will speak it out of my mouth
I am more than a conqueror

I do not have the spirit of fear
I have the victory
No weapon formed against me will prosper
In His Name, the devil has to flee

God will not lie
If He said it I believe
He will open up the windows of heaven
And pour out blessings that I won't have
room to receive

I am healed by His stripes
I shall live and not die
I rebuke the enemy
I plead the blood over my life

I am above and not beneath
I am the first and not the last
I am the child of the Most High
I am not my past

Lisa Bradley
BE ENCOURAGED

I have the authority to tread on serpents
I have the ability to crush them
I know nothing can hurt me
I am greater because of Him

My words have power
Therefore, I speak life

Lisa Bradley
BE ENCOURAGED

THE LORD IS

When I need to be encouraged and lifted up
The Lord is my <u>S</u>TRENGTH

When I am completely lost and alone
The Lord is my <u>H</u>OPE

When I feel empty and unsure
The Lord is my <u>E</u>TERNITY

When my mind needs that stillness beyond understanding
The Lord is my <u>P</u>EACE

When I am attacked physically and mentally
The Lord is my <u>H</u>EALER

When I am troubled and see no way out
The Lord is my <u>E</u>XODUS

When I am scared and need a place to hide
The Lord is my <u>R</u>EFUGE

When I am struggling and weighted down
The Lord is my <u>D</u>ELIVERER

The Lord is all I need
He is my <u>SHEPHERD</u>

THE POWER OF THE OIL

My Head His Covering
My Mind His Thoughts
My Face His Light
The Power of the Oil

My Eyes His Vision
My Ears His Voice
My Nose His Fragrance
The Power of the Oil

My Hands His Touch
My Mouth His Words
My Shoulders His Strength
The Power of the Oil

My Lungs His Breath
My Veins His Blood
My Heart His Love
The Power of the Oil

My Feet His Walk
My Steps His Order
My Body His Temple
The Power of the Oil

Lisa Bradley
BE ENCOURAGED

My Soul His Joy
My Flesh His Spirit
My Desires His Will
The Power of the Oil

My Life His Reflection
My Existence His Presence
My Purpose His Anointing
The Power of the Oil

My Natural His Supernatural
That's the Power of the Oil

The Power of the Oil II
(A WOMAN'S BLESSING)

Blessed is her head as the covering for His
Glory
Even as her hairs turn gray, she will continue
to tell her story

Blessed is her mind to keep His thoughts
Even when she is confronted with confusion
and self-doubts

Blessed is her face to shine with His light
Even as she battles with the terrors of the
night

Blessed are her ears to hear His voice
As she tries to block out the distractions of
the noise

Blessed are her eyes to see His vision
Even through the attacks of the enemy trying
to delay His mission

Blessed is her mouth to speak His word
Even in those times when she feels as though
she's not being heard

Lisa Bradley
BE ENCOURAGED

Blessed are her shoulders to bare His strength
Even when the weight of this world has her
spent

Blessed are her hands to share His touch
Showing others that He loves us just that
much

Blessed is her heart to beat with His love
unconditionally
Even when she's been challenged and tested
spiritually

Blessed are her lungs to inhale His breath
As He gave her life through His Son's death

Blessed are her veins as the Blood of Jesus
runs through it
Flowing as a river and pumping like a
transfusion

Blessed is her soul to carry the joy of the Lord
Even when life's trials make the way seem so
hard

Blessed are her desires to line up with His
will

Lisa Bradley
BE ENCOURAGED

While waiting on Him patiently and keeping
still

Blessed is her life to be a mirror image of His
reflection
As she's being led and guided by His
direction

Blessed she is from the crown to the sole
And may He keep her temple whole

VICTIM TO VICTOR

Depression
Was the diagnosis that they gave
But unbeknownst to them
God already had the plan made

From hospital to hospital
One pill to another
The struggle was real and deep
But God knew how long she would suffer

No one ever truly understood
Being picked on as a teen
Fighting from the bullying
School was a tough scene

Tired and exhausted
Not understanding the emotions
Finding it hard to go on
Yet never questioned His motives

Holding on for dear life
On this rollercoaster ride
Knowing at some point
She would have to get off and let Him be her
guide

Completely submitting

Lisa Bradley
BE ENCOURAGED

To His will and His call
Preparing to fully yield and lay down
Succumbing and surrendering all

Was a victim of the enemy
Wounded and scarred
But came out a victor
With the help of the Lord

YOUR SEASON IS NOW

Your Season is now
The delay was only a test
Satan's agenda has been cancelled
God is about to show you His very best

Your season is now
He is sending you a mighty release
Of what was held up and held back
Because you stood firm in your belief

Your season is now
God has been equipping you for this all along
He is closing the mouths of your naysayers
Because you didn't faint, never doubted and
held on

Your season is now
Get ready to be set free
God's set up will be an upset
For all of your enemies

Your season is now
You waited patiently for your time
You remained faithful and continued to pray
And for that God is about to blow your mind

Lisa Bradley
BE ENCOURAGED

Your season is now
Breakthroughs, miracles and restoration
God has paved the way
To lead you to your ordained destination

Your season is now
There is no limit to what God is going to do
He promised it so get ready to receive
All that He has planned for you

Your season is now
God is going to show you His ultimate favor
You've sown in fertile ground
So it's time to see the fruits of your labor

Your season is now
Your vision is about to manifest
Prepare yourself for the abundance
Because it's time to reap the harvest

Yes, your season is now

About The Author

Lisa Bradley was born and raised in Bishopville, South Carolina to Viola Shaw and the late Charlie Shaw. She is the eldest of two children. She is married to Mathis Bradley and together they have one daughter, Alisha. After graduating from Lee County public schools, she went on to receive an Associate Degree in Computer Technology from Sumter Area Technical College, a Bachelor of Science in Organizational Management from Morris College and a Master's from Webster University in Educational Technology.

She has authored such books as Expressions of the Heart Inspirational Poems, Expressions of the Heart Word Search, God's World Poetry for Kids and God's World Activity Book. She also has an inspirational poetry CD.

Lisa started writing later in life than most. Putting pen to paper for family and friends and then realizing that although the purpose for her writing may have started for others, in the end, it was for her. A way to deal with her family's challenges with depression, it became a way of escape. And in doing so, she knew God gave her this gift to share with others. Her prayer is that if one person is inspired, uplifted or encouraged by one word, then it is all worth it.